The
RIGHT
WORDS
for Hard
Times

new seasons®

Emily Thornton Calvo, a freelance writer, has more than 15 years of experience in both writing and marketing—and even more years offering comforting words of consolation. Calvo has a BA from Loyola University and writes from Chicago.

Marie D. Jones is an ordained minister and a contributing author to numerous books, including *Echoes of Love: Sisters, Mother, Grandmother, Friends, Graduation, Wedding; Mother's Daily Prayer Book,* and *When You Lose Someone You Love: A Year of Comfort.* She is the creator/producer of Gigglebug Farms Simply Storybook children's videos.

Ellen F. Pill is a writer who has contributed to several inspirational books, including *Blessed by an Angel* and *Echoes of Love: Baby.* In addition, her stories and sentiments have been published in *Whispers from Heaven* magazine, as well as in American Greetings and Hallmark cards.

Unless otherwise noted, Scripture quotations are taken from the *New Revised Standard Version* of the Bible. Copyright © 1989 by the Division of Christian Education of the National Council of the Churches of Christ in the USA. Used by Permission. All rights reserved.

Scripture quotations marked NIV are taken from *The Holy Bible, New International Version.* Copyright © 1973, 1978, 1984, International Bible Society. Used by permission of Zondervan Publishing House. All rights reserved.

Photo credits:

Front and back cover: © **Sharon K. Broutzas**

Artville Collection: 58, 67; © **Sharon K. Broutzas:** 17, 18, 32, 42, 50, 54, 64; **Corbis Collection:** 12; **Digital Vision Collection:** 30, 35; **Eyewire Collection:** 21, 24, 27; **Good Shoot Nature Collection:** 53; **PhotoDisc Collection:** 9, 11, 15, 23, 29, 36, 39, 46, 49, 57, 61, 63, 71, 75, 77; **StockByte Collection:** 41, 45, 68, 72.

New Seasons is a registered trademark of Publications International, Ltd.

© 2006 New Seasons
All rights reserved.
This publication may not be reproduced in whole or in part by any means whatsoever without written permission from:

Louis Weber, CEO
Publications International, Ltd.
7373 North Cicero Avenue
Lincolnwood, Illinois 60712

www.pilbooks.com

Permission is never granted for commercial purposes.

Manufactured in China.

8 7 6 5 4 3 2 1

ISBN-13: 978-1-4127-5535-1
ISBN-10: 1-4127-5535-2

Contents

Finding the Right Words

When friends or loved ones face troubles or suffer a painful loss, they need support and encouragement. Yet those circumstances are often the ones that cause awkwardness. People around them have a difficult time finding the right words to say. Uncomfortable with the pain and sadness, they withdraw and are unable to respond when it's needed most.

The Right Words for Hard Times provides the messages you need to convey warmth, encouragement, and support. These messages are the keys to expressing your feelings with grace and concern. Whether a good friend or family member experiences a job loss, an illness, a turbulent divorce, or the death of a loved one, *The Right Words for Hard Times* has the perfect message to write in a card or say in person.

Each chapter addresses a specific situation and contains a variety of greetings that are appropriate for familiar relationships as well as more formal ones. Some messages

are deeply inspirational while others lend light-hearted cheer. All are sensitive responses that help you feel comfortable sharing your feelings. Keep *The Right Words for Hard Times* handy so that when you need to write a quick note or send an e-mail, you'll have a wealth of suitable responses ready for any sad occasion. You can also give the book as a gift to help those around you handle those difficult times with equal grace and compassion.

The Right Words for Hard Times contains the messages that we find so difficult to express, which, when shared, will say volumes about you.

Words of Comfort

May this setback bring a life that is richer than before.

Enclosed: One giant hug to help make things easier.

My heart reaches out to you at this painful time, offering love, comfort, and friendship.

If I listed all the instances of a setback leading to happy results, this message would go on forever. So look for the silver lining and be at peace.

May the day come when you look back on this time and laugh.

Look up "cope" in the dictionary, and read about yourself.

Open our eyes, dear Lord,
That we may see
The far vast reaches of eternity.
Help us to look beyond life's
    little cares
So prone to fret us
And the grief that wears
Our courage thin.
O may we tune our hearts
To Thy great harmony
That all the parts may ever be
In perfect, sweet accord.
Give us Thine own clear vision,
    blessed Lord.

—CORRIE TEN BOOM
EACH NEW DAY

No one can truly understand how difficult this time is for you, but you have our love and prayers.

Boredom can be the state of monotony caused by things constantly going well. May things get boring really soon.

When I recall all that you have done for me when I needed you, I realize how much I owe you. It's time for you to collect. Let me help.

This is a time when you discover who your friends are, and I want you to know you can count on me.

Tough times give us the lessons and the inner strength to create happier days.

The perfect antidote to troubles is a sense of humor. Don't forget that!

It's time to take off your sackcloth, dust off the penitential ashes, and get on with seeing to it that your life is full of meaning from here on out. You'll not change what happened before ... and the quickest way to change your attitude is to stop flogging yourself.

—JACK MUMMEY

I hope my words will help you once again feel joy and hope. For now, I just want you to know how much I care.

God never intended us to know everything, but He will reveal to us all we need to know. If we knew and understood everything, we'd have no need for faith. In our own minds and hearts, God would be diminished. Some things we're not able to understand anyway, and some things are best left unknown. So in His time, God may disclose some things to us, but in some instances, His love gift may be silence. The most important thing to remember is that we never walk alone.

—FRAN CAFFEY SANDIN
TOUCHING THE CLOUDS

There's always a little bit of heaven in a disaster. May you soon discover your bit of heaven.

Take a deep breath, think of all the people who care about you, and know that you can get through this.

Life may be like a bowl of cherries, but sometimes it's full of pits.

If your days seem too long to
   cope with,
And your nights too dark to bear,
There is someone who cares very
   deeply.
Just call me, and I'll be there.

We send our love and heartfelt
prayers across the miles that you
may find the strength you need to
get through each day.

In grief our hearts, filled with our
   plight,
Forget the day that follows night.
But faith alone can shine the light
That leads us into pastures bright.

No matter how heavy the burden,
God will be there to share the load
you carry.

My heart goes out to you; my
spirit prays for you; my love
surrounds you. Though I cannot be
with you in person, my friendship is
always with you.

'Tis but a part we see, and not
a whole.

—Alexander Pope
"An Essay on Man"

If you need a friend to talk to or
just someone to sit with in silence,
I am here.

Life is never easy, and sometimes
it challenges us in ways we think
we are not capable of overcoming.
But we are capable, and we can
overcome. I believe in you.

God made friends so that in times like these, we have someone to talk to, lean on, and mourn with. I am here for you, my friend.

⟋⟍

Man was made for Joy & Woe,
And when this we rightly know
Thro the World we safely go.

—WILLIAM BLAKE
"AUGURIES OF INNOCENCE"

⟋⟍

I send love and prayers to surround you when you are feeling lost and alone. No matter how far away I may be, you are always close to my heart.

⟋⟍

May you find comfort and peace to carry you through each day. May you find faith and hope to keep you strong until this difficult time is over.

Whatever you are seeking, know that he will help you find it. I pray for you—for guidance and peace.

⟋⟍

Is there anything I can do to help ease your pain? If so, don't be afraid or ashamed to let me know. I sincerely want to help.

⟋⟍

Through good times and bad, I am here for you, friend. Through bright days and dark, you can count on me.

⟋⟍

If you need someone to help you get through this, know that I will be there at a moment's notice.

⟋⟍

The right words can be so hard to find. Simply know that I'm thinking of you every moment.

I believe in you—
in your wisdom,
in your courage,
in your strength.
I believe in you.

Yet, in the maddening maze
   of things,
And tossed by storm and flood,
To one fixed trust my spirit clings;
I know that God is good!

—JOHN GREENLEAF WHITTIER
"ETERNAL GOODNESS"

May you find everything you
need to see you through these
difficult moments. And if there
is something you don't find,
please ask.

All you have to do is call. I can
be there anytime. I want so very
much to help.

Believe in yourself. Believe in
the Lord. Believe that everything
will be okay. Believe . . .

Look to this very moment—
touch it, sense it, feel it, and know
that you are blessed and that he
will guide you to exactly where
you need to be.

Job Trouble

Caring support is only a phone call away.

Bigger and better things are in store, for unexpected happiness awaits you.

They say that good things come to those who persevere, so I know you'll soon experience good things.

Don't worry—downsizing often leads to upsizing a career!

When problems on the job seem too much to deal with, remember that you are bigger than your job and stronger than your problems.

Don't worry. I have faith that you will find the perfect job and enjoy every success.

A challenge is a victory in progress.

I am incredibly proud of you and the work that you're doing. You are an amazing example of what life is all about.

When I said, "My foot is slipping," your love, O Lord, supported me. When anxiety was great within me, your consolation brought joy to my soul.

PSALM 94:18–19 NIV

Things may be rough right now, but it will get better. Hang in there.

Sometimes we confuse what we do for a living with who we are. Don't let this job get to you. You are so much more than a job title.

Look around. I'm behind you!

One lost opportunity is a sure sign that a better one is on the horizon.

Change seems exceedingly frightening at first, but it holds the key to transformation and the joy of finding a strength we never knew we had.

Hope springs eternal in the
   human breast:
Man never Is, but always
   To be blest.
   —ALEXANDER POPE
   "ESSAY ON MAN"

When things fall apart, they usually come together in a new way. Look forward to the doors that are now opening to you, where none existed before.

Change is never easy, but the love of family and friends makes it just a little easier to bear.

~

I know how much losing this job means to you, but I also know in my heart that you are strong, resourceful, and talented enough to land on your feet.

~

Walking away from a job that gave you security is never easy, but remember that you are walking toward a better opportunity to be all you were meant to be.

~

Remember that you are not your job. You are someone capable of achieving your dreams. I believe in you and in your dreams.

When you pass through the waters, I will be with you; and through the rivers, they shall not overwhelm you; when you walk through fire you shall not be burned, and the flame shall not consume you.

ISAIAH 43:2

~

Stay safe until the Lord leads you back home.

Remember, it's only a job.

I know it isn't easy right now, but you are doing his work and that is everything. I'm thinking about you and praying for you every day.

Behind every obstacle is a golden opportunity to spring forward into a future filled with exciting new possibilities.

A job is just a place we go to for a paycheck. I wish for you a vocation—a powerful calling that brings out the gifts you were born to express.

Believe in tomorrow, and let faith guide you through today.

I hope the future brings you a new job where you can really spread your wings and use the many gifts and talents God has given you.

There is a job out there just perfect for the person you are in your heart of hearts. I pray you find that job.

God has a bigger, bolder, better plan for you. Don't worry about losing this job. You will find another even more suited to you.

Your day-to-day life must be so difficult right now. Just get safely through each day, and remember that you are loved.

Let the love of family and friends guide you through each day until you find a place where you can breathe easy and relax once again.

It's hard to keep a sunny outlook when your job situation is painfully difficult each day. Remember that you're there for a reason and that there are people who care!

What matters most is that you *stay active*, that you stay focused on your goals for the future. As you move forward, you will discover destinations you never thought about before. You can then decide where, among these destinations, you would like to go.

—ARTHUR FREEMAN AND ROSE DEWOLF
WOULDA/COULDA/SHOULDA

It's tough when your work isn't satisfying. Try to fill the other hours with good things and good people, and you'll see this through!

Hoping that you can sense our prayers and that they help protect you every day until you are safely home.

You've lost your job, but you haven't lost your friends. I'm with you on this. Just tell me what I can do to help!

Your strength is an inspiration. Your courage is a challenge for the rest of us. What you do day to day, I can't even imagine in my dreams. Stay safe.

Losing a job can be really disruptive—personally, professionally, financially. It might seem as if everything is changing, but no matter what—I'm here for you.

So often we identify ourselves through our work, but I just want to remind you that you're terrific no matter what is happening in your 9 to 5 world!

You *are* going to move into a job that makes you want to get up each morning. I just know it! Hang in there.

God is our refuge and strength, an ever-present help in trouble. Therefore we will not fear.

PSALM 46:1–2 NIV

J.O.B.—Just Old Business. Hang in there, get through it, and you'll be on your way to something better soon.

Financial Woes

Sweet are the uses of adversity,
Which, like the toad, ugly and
venomous,
Wears yet a precious jewel in his
head.

—WILLIAM SHAKESPEARE
AS YOU LIKE IT

Money is such a sensitive issue, but it shouldn't be among good friends. If you are having problems, please let me help.

When times are tough, remember that you are far more resourceful than you realize. May you find the inner strength to see you through this challenge.

Come to me, all you who are weary and burdened, and I will give you rest.

MATTHEW 11:28 NIV

It's difficult to see how something positive can come from something so painful, but with time you will see opportunities for growth if you keep your faith strong.

Be grateful, for you still have your health upon which to build your future.

You worked hard and came a long way. Don't worry; you'll do it again.

When your problems consume you, that is the time to focus instead on the blessings of life all around you. May this new perspective give you hope.

Peace of mind has no price tag.

You have the love and respect of family and friends. Despite your financial woes, you still have what is far more important.

The hill, though high, I covet to
  ascend,
The difficulty will not me offend;
For I perceive the way to life lies
  here.
Come, pluck up my heart, let's
  neither faint nor fear...

—JOHN BUNYAN
THE PILGRIM'S PROGRESS

Rough spots happen to everyone now and again, and they can be tough to handle. The one good thing is that they make the times of smooth sailing seem twice as sweet!

When money woes threaten to derail our peace of mind, it helps to remember that we are blessed with gifts and talents so we can prosper again.

A financial setback always feels less significant after a shopping spree at the dollar store.

You have the kind of character that is always able to bounce back. I look forward to seeing you bounce back soon.

Right now, life must seem like such a huge mountain to climb, but I know you're going to do it, because I've seen you make it through tough spots before. You're amazing.

May your openness and peaceful conduct inspire the generosity of others toward you.

Please have faith that you'll make it through this: faith in yourself, faith in the people who care about you, and, most of all, faith in God, for he is always by your side.

During life's trials, we can rest assured that God loves us. Nothing we do can make Him love us more. Nothing we do can make Him love us less. His love is unchanging, unfailing, everlasting.

—Fran Caffey Sandin
Touching the Clouds

This is a difficult time for you, but remember you don't have to go through it alone.

Life has its ups and downs, and those involving money can be so stressful. Let me know how I can help.

When you think there is simply not enough money to make ends meet, God will find a way to make up the difference.

In our greatest challenges we find our greatest opportunities. I pray your challenges lead to newfound blessings for you and your family.

When the challenges you face seem to be more than you can handle, know that I will come to help lighten your burden in any way I can.

Friendship means sticking together in good times and in bad. I am here for you, no matter how tough a time you are having.

Sometimes talking about money can be difficult, even embarrassing. But I am your friend, and I am here to listen and to support you in any way I can.

I hope your money troubles are over soon and that you are back on your feet and ready to take life on again with newfound hope and energy.

May God give you the strength and the courage to deal with the terrible misfortune that has befallen you.

Prosperity is not without many fears and distastes; and adversity is not without comforts and hopes.

—Francis Bacon
"Of Adversity"

You can recover from this and find financial stability again. It will take time and perseverance, but you can do it. And I'm here to help—any way that I can.

Take a deep breath, and allow yourself to know that everything will truly be all right.

Know that in time and with faith the financial obstacles you now face will vanish and life will be an abundance of blessings again.

Keep walking with the Lord, and soon your steps will be firm, confident, and sure once again.

Remember your dreams—hold them tight—for they will lift you up even if the world seems to be pushing you down.

Each day is a challenge. Face it head on, and rock the world with your strength!

In the stillness of your soul, may you find a quiet peace where you can let go of the problems you face and renew your spirit.

I guess bad things do happen to good people, because you're about the best person ever. I'm praying for you and wondering if there's anything I can do to help you.

Money can cause so many headaches, but it's not everything. You have a lot of people who are pulling for you and want to help you get through this. Look to God for gentle guidance, for he will lead you through these difficult times.

The Lord is my shepherd, I shall not want. He makes me lie down in green pastures, he leads me beside quiet waters, he restores my soul.

PSALM 23:1–3 NIV

I heard about your situation, and I'm so sorry this had to happen. I have everyone I know praying for you!

Financial Woes

Depression and Loneliness

I see hope as a daily process of looking for something to feel good about. Every single day I try to find something to be grateful for— maybe that my father is still with us, that I'm learning more about how to be a better caregiver, or that I can still say "I love you" even if he seems not to be listening.... No matter what happens, I still hold onto a strong sense that something positive will come from all of this.

—LEONARD FELDER
WHEN A LOVED ONE IS ILL

God will be there in your darkest hours to walk with you. You are not alone.

What can I do for you in this time of need? Cook you a warm dinner? Share a memory? Be someone you can lean on? Whatever helps, you can count on me.

Don't fret. You're sure to find the person who is right for you.

Look for the sunrise in the morning. Look for the moon and stars at night. In these places, you will see the possibility of a new day and find hope.

Where there's life, there's hope, and you have an abundance of life.

Life is about change, so live in the moment and find joy because anything can happen next.

I always try to surround myself with good people, and I never had to look further than you.

When the road ahead seems impassable and the obstacles insurmountable, that is when God will be there to carry you.

When you feel hopeless, remember that God loves you dearly.
When you feel useless, remember that God has a plan for you.

A cheerful heart is a good medicine.

PROVERBS 17:22

Keep your eyes on the light ahead and your heart on God's promise that he will be there to help you no matter how bad things may seem.

When things fall apart, it feels as though we will never recover. But know that everything does come together again when we reach out to those who care for us.

There is a new dawn awaiting you at the end of this long, dark night. Hold fast to your faith, your hope, and your dreams. You will get there.

Though the road facing you may seem impassable, know that the light of God's love is there to clear your path and guide you along the way.

With time, there will be a brighter day for you. I pray that the darkness will soon clear and the light of life's blessings will quickly heal your spirit.

Even when the day looks gray, remember that it's always sunny above the clouds.

No coward soul is mine
No trembler in the world's
    storm-troubled sphere
I see Heaven's glories shine
And Faith shines equal arming
    me from Fear.

—EMILY JANE BRONTË

I'm sorry I can't be with you, but I'm sending you my prayers of comfort and of hope.

$\mathcal{I}$ pray that the fog of this depression soon lifts, revealing clear, blue skies again.

$\mathcal{A}$lone, we stumble headlong into
   the night,
But with God's grace we walk in
   loving light.

$\mathcal{W}$hat can you do when everything seems lost? Find the place inside of you where all is still, and listen for the voice that whispers of hope.

$\mathcal{H}$ope is a lover's staff; walk hence
   with that,
And manage it against despairing
   thoughts.

—WILLIAM SHAKESPEARE
THE TWO GENTLEMEN OF VERONA

$\mathcal{W}$hen you feel as though no one cares or understands, know that I do and that I am always here to talk or just to listen.

$\mathcal{I}$f you ever feel so alone that you think you cannot go on, promise me you will pick up the phone and call me.

$\mathcal{I}$f it all gets too confusing and stressful, just stop for a moment.
   Breathe.
   Breathe.
   Breathe.
   There. Now call me, and we'll
      talk. I'm here. And I care.

$\mathcal{W}$hen your heart feels a chill, let God warm you from the inside out!

You are not alone. Even though we are far apart, my heart is there with you, now and always.

When life looks bleak and hopeless, hold fast to your faith in God, for he can lift you out of the darkness.

God is with you during this difficult time…and so am I.

Praying that you find peace and hope tucked into the quiet places of each day.

"Hope" is the thing with
    feathers—
That perches in the soul—
And sings the tune without the
    words—
And never stops—at all—

—EMILY DICKINSON

Tomorrow will come and, with it, a lightness and peace that you may not yet imagine.

Don't look back to where you've been. Look ahead to a brand new day—a time when everything is coming up roses. They are absolutely beautiful!

Be strong and courageous.
Do not be terrified; do not be
discouraged, for the Lord your God
will be with you wherever you go.

—Joshua 1:9 NIV

If you need a hand, a shoulder,
an ear, a hug—anything at all—I'm
right beside you.

Please remember—you are not
alone. I'm right here with you every
step of the way. Even when you
don't see me beside you, I'm with
you in thought, in heart, in mind.

Even in the total darkness, when
our eyes adjust, we can see what
we need to see. Look around, and
know that you are not alone.

Believe in yourself. Believe in life.
Believe that the Lord will lead you
to better days.

In the dark times, all it takes is
the tiniest of lights to lead us to
tomorrow. Look to his light.

Whene'er the fate of those I hold
    most dear
Tells to my fearful breast a tale of
    sorrow,
O bright-eyed Hope, my morbid
    fancy cheer;
Let me awhile thy sweetest
    comforts borrow.

—John Keats
"To Hope"

When you're feeling lonely, please
call me. I'll be with you in a flash!

Bruised Relationships

Possibly someday you both will be close friends.

I just wanted to let you know how much I care about you. When you are ready to talk, I will be ready to listen.

Dealing with others can be difficult, especially when there is hurt and anger involved. I pray that you all find a resolution you can live with.

I know what a tough time you've been having. If you want to talk about it, I'm here for you.

With clenched fists, I had been holding on to the hope that one day, the man who changed my life forever by his selfish act would feel remorse and that his remorse would make my life all better. I had thought that his confession of guilt would be the day I forgave the crime and moved on. But I realized that forgiveness was not dependent on his remorse. Forgiveness was my choice and it was for me. I would forgive for my sake.

When there is forgiveness, there is a chance to move forward.

—ME RA KOH
BEAUTY RESTORED

I pray that healing is taking place for you in your relationships and that you find peace and harmony in all your affairs.

Forgive. It's God's way. Let it also be yours.

Being on the outs with someone you really care about is hard. Just know that time, patience, and forgiveness will one day heal the rift between you.

People are so different, and sometimes our differences can make us crazy. But know that there is common ground you can tread, where the hope of reconciliation is waiting.

May God's love fill you with hope, healing, and the forgiveness needed to resolve the personal struggles you are dealing with.

Sometimes, we tend to respond poorly to trying circumstances because we think we deserve better. Our society and media tell us that everybody should be happy, comfortable, healthy, and successful. The difficulty arises when we believe these statements.

—ROBERT S. MCGEE
THE SEARCH FOR SIGNIFICANCE

Pray for guidance, and God will help you mend this relationship.

Hurtful relationships can cause so much stress. Let me know how I can help you make sense of this unfortunate situation.

When someone we trusted betrays us, we often lose faith in everyone. But don't lose faith or hope in everyone just because of what one person did.

"O dreary life!" we cry, "O dreary life!"
And still the generations of the birds
Sing through our sighing, and the flocks and herds
Serenely live while we are keeping strife.

—ELIZABETH BARRETT BROWNING
"PATIENCE TAUGHT BY NATURE"

If someone hurts you, turn the other cheek. If they insult you, smile back and offer them love. Compassion can heal what confrontation cannot.

Patching up a relationship is difficult after so many harsh words have been exchanged. But with God's help, you can both learn to forgive and move on.

I pray that you find reconciliation with your family soon and that you can all find it in your hearts to come together again in forgiveness and compassion.

Taking the first step is always the hardest, and now that you've done it, you're well on your way.

The God who seems absent will come to us again. It is an enormous comfort to me to have discovered that, in some way I may not expect, God will initiate, breaking into chaos with blessing.

—Patricia H. Livingston
This Blessed Mess

Don't let the small differences between you destroy your friendship. It's the big things you two have in common that make your relationship worthwhile. So take your eyes off the small things, and focus on the big things.

Even those closest to us can hurt us. But love is stronger than anger. Let love heal the wounds between you and your family.

We're given life. Then we're given the ability to choose to create warmth and goodness between us. It isn't always easy, but it's always the right thing to do.

In the trying times, remember what a blessing family is. Think of good and happy memories, and imagine how much you'd miss them. Then make the first move toward reconciliation and forgiveness.

When you speak the truth in a loving way, you have taken a huge step toward peace.

Let go of the stress and the hurt, and remember that we're all doing our very best to help.

It's hard to be the one to say "Enough!" when relationships grow tense, but someone has to be strong enough and wise enough. That someone can be you.

In families where recovery is successful, a truly new life may begin. Parents and children will find a new affection in their understanding and trust of each other, a new depth in their open communication with each other. This is the true goal of the whole process of treatment.... One survivor felt he had been blessed by this whole new life. "Thank God," he said. "I just might have missed knowing and appreciating life as it is now."

—VERNON E. JOHNSON
I'LL QUIT TOMORROW

Sometimes it seems so hard to get from here to there. You know where to go; the trick is to take the first step.

When there is healing to do, call on God's wisdom, his guidance, and his love.

Sometimes the expectations of others lead to bad feelings and hurtful situations. I wish you the experience of peace in all your relationships.

Just keep following your heart, and you will know which way to turn.

Breaking Up

The past gives us the opportunity to learn. The future gives us the opportunity to live.

Like a summer day approaching evening, love—once warm—can cool down, forcing us to move on. May your journey be filled with the warmth of a future love.

The ending of a relationship always seems unsettling. But once we come out the other side, we realize it was what we needed to grow and evolve.

Savor being single again. It may not last long.

Sometimes a bad spouse can make an excellent "Ex." May you both eventually find the relationship that works.

It's not failure—only change, awakening, and courage.

I hold it true, whate'er befall;
I feel it, when I sorrow most;
'Tis better to have loved and lost
Than never to have loved at all.

—ALFRED LORD TENNYSON
"IN MEMORIAM"

Ending a relationship is difficult. Kudos to you for exemplifying grace.

Married, divorced, or separated—whatever your status, you can still live happily ever after.

May every day bring you closer to loving again.

When love isn't enough, someone to lean on can be just what you need. I'm here to listen whenever you need to talk.

Unhappy marriages can make one look unattractive. Congratulations on the makeover.

Forgive, so you can move on and feel happier. But don't forget, or you're bound to repeat the experience.

Living with bitterness is like taking work with you on vacation. It's time to embrace the joy and fun!

Whenever you're ready, love will be around the corner waiting for your warmth and passion.

Now you can enjoy the relaxed peace of mind that marriage should have brought your life. May you live happily ever after.

Here's to looking forward to the future! May your divorce be the beginning of greater happiness.

Congratulations on rehabbing your life!

As for losses and gains, we have seen how often they are inextricably mixed. There is plenty we have to give up in order to grow. For we cannot deeply love anything without becoming vulnerable to loss. And we cannot become separate people, responsible people, connected people, reflective people, without some losing and leaving and letting go.

—Judith Viorst
Necessary Losses

Here's to learning that you are your own better half.

Congratulations, for you win custody of our friendship. I'm here for you.

He heals the brokenhearted, and binds up their wounds.

PSALM 147:3

Yes, you can talk to your divorce attorney, but I'm cheaper. Call me whenever you need to talk.

As one door closes, another waits to be opened. I am here to support you as you walk into your new life.

Here's to decorating your place without any negotiation.

Letting go of a relationship can feel like losing a part of your self. In time, you will feel whole again and ready to start anew. Give yourself that time.

Just call if you need a friend to talk with, to lean on, or to cry to. I am here for you.

A spouse is not a necessity for happiness! Congratulations on your singlehood.

The sadness that you now feel will one day turn to new joy and new opportunities to love. Keep hope alive in your heart.

I pray that God's love will be the soothing balm you need to heal the wounds of your divorce.

Just wanted you to know that although love relationships may come and go, our friendship will last forever.

This life may seem as though it is ending, but I believe in you and in your courage to see the new life that waits ahead.

Divorce is not a mistake made but a lesson learned. Take the wisdom you have gleaned, and apply it to the rest of your life.

Faith is the power that heals all suffering and moves us toward new horizons of love and happiness. Have faith that those horizons are within reach.

I pray that this tragic situation does not make you lose your faith in love. Keep your heart open and your love alive. Life can be a miracle again.

When you divorce, you not only part with a spouse, you also leave behind your past, your whole way of life, the future plans and expectations you once had, and a good chunk of your identity. Part of the letting-go process is mourning your losses and the death of your marriage, just as you mourn the death of a person who has been an important part of your life. Once a death is mourned, the pain eases, memories of the departed person lose their power to provoke tears and sorrow, and the mourner feels that he or she can let go of the past and get on with life once again. This is what happens when people mourn the death of their marriage.

—Genevieve Clapp
Divorce and New Beginnings

Everything must seem so complicated, but you've got a friend right here, waiting with a hand, shoulder, ear—whatever it takes to make the world a little easier to understand.

The life you were living has changed so very much. Yet I believe in you and know that you will build a new life surrounded by the love of family and friends.

We've all heard that when a door slams in our face, somewhere a window opens. Search for that window, and seek out the breeze. It's there! Truly, it is.

Love isn't gone forever. It's merely waiting in the wings for the time when you are ready once again.

Count on the love and support of family and friends to see you through this...and that definitely means ME!

I've been down this road myself, so I know how uneven the path can be. I also know that step by step, it does get better.

Repeat after me: I deserve better.

Write a letter to your former mate (it never needs to be mailed) thanking him or her for all the gifts you received from your marriage. Having a written record of the benefits you derived from your marriage and an acknowledgement of your former spouse's contribution to them is not a bad idea. It will not only dissipate your resentments, but in the future it will allow you to view your marriage from a fresh and positive perspective.

—GENEVIEVE CLAPP
DIVORCE AND NEW BEGINNINGS

You've got friends on your side—friends who want to help and who'll see you through this mess—no matter what!

The good times together were a gift; the hard times, an education. Happy graduation.

Love, like life, is fraught with changes. I pray that the end of this relationship opens the door to something even better. You deserve it.

Saying goodbye to a marriage and a way of life is painful for everyone. If you need someone to talk to, just call me anytime. I'm here for you.

Even when it doesn't seem like it, always remember that although it will take a lot to get through this, you definitely have what it takes!

Your heart is breaking now, but time will heal the wound and bring you new reasons to love again.

Have faith in God's wisdom, and know that, difficult as it may seem, you are right where you are supposed to be.

You made a huge life change—a leap of faith—so hold on and let God lead the way to better times.

What you did took incredible strength and courage and faith. You're pretty amazing!

When things don't always turn out the way we've imagined, we just have to have faith in the Lord's wisdom and guidance, belief in the future, and trust that he will show the way.

Fairy tale endings can seem so out of reach. But please remember, there is still magic in this world.

Upside down…inside out…life shifts and changes…often in totally unexpected ways. Keep your faith, for he is with you, and there is always a reason. With God, you can handle anything!

Stick with your decision. It was the right thing to do.

Times of Illness

Living with a terminal prognosis of a loved one is painful.... In the midst of stumbling along this unchosen path, there is one small consolation: You have been given a final gift of time to adapt to this drastic change. With advance warning, you have an opportunity to make plans, help get legal issues in order and find out the patient's wishes for final arrangements. You have been given the chance to say good-bye, to express your love, to tie up loose ends and to make amends.

—JUNE CERZA KOLF
COMFORT & CARE IN A FINAL ILLNESS

Having your health is great, but when you don't, a group of people who care can make you feel a lot better. We're thinking of you.

In times like these, sometimes it helps to go off by yourself, recharge, and come out fighting. Good luck, and good health.

God whispers to us in our pleasures, speaks in our conscience, but shouts in our pains: it is His megaphone to rouse a deaf world.

—C. S. LEWIS
THE PROBLEM OF PAIN

You are stronger than this illness that has left your body weak. With the love and support of those who care, you will find healing and wholeness again.

Though you may be suffering now, know that deep within a powerful healing is taking place and that God's grace and love is shining down upon you.

Every day I say a prayer for you—a prayer for well-being and health. A prayer that each day will be better than the last. A prayer for your recovery.

I'm in my fifties now and, with it, I am facing a whole new set of aches and pains, limitations and challenges. But rather than worry about the future . . . I'll keep trusting God one day at a time. I will say "yes" to the offer of his strength and power and "no" to grumbling, no matter if I face a four-week stint in bed with pressure sores, or a flat tire on my wheelchair when I'm cruising the Thousand Oaks mall.

—JONI EARECKSON TADA
TODAY'S HEROES

May God's healing touch be upon you. May God's loving spirit be within you.

Sending prayers of healing for your body, mind, and spirit that you may become even stronger than before.

Hoping that you find a glimmer of goodness in every day to help you cope with your illness.

Faith will get you through this difficult time, but should your faith in God waver, know in your heart that his faith in you never does.

There is a peace that passes all understanding, and that peace is always available to you as you deal with this difficult experience.

Let the Lord be your comfort and your strength during this time of healing. Let his love embrace you as a loving parent holds a child.

I know that you are going through a difficult time dealing with your illness. I pray that you experience a positive healing and brighter days ahead.

Rather than running from or resenting your suffering, would you be willing to look for God in it? Would you allow suffering to lead you to the very heart of God, a place where you can find the comfort and peace that you crave as well as the hope that has the power to transform your tomorrows?...God wants to use the difficulties in your life not to punish you or to hurt you but to draw you to himself. Will you come?

—NANCY GUTHRIE
HOLDING ON TO HOPE

Even as your body seems to fail you, remember how powerful your spirit is and how blessed your heart is. You'll get through this.

I pray for you to get well sooner than soon, stronger than strong, and to come out of this experience more resilient than ever before.

The curse of steady good health is that your well-established routines make you forget that some things are more important than others. Illness' blessing is that the relative importance of things will become clear to you again....It's time to transform your acknowledged mortality into deliberate, artful living. Select every act as carefully as you'd select dishes from the menu of a fine restaurant you'll visit only once.

—JEFF KANE
BE SICK WELL

One day her husband said to me, "I don't know why she is still alive.... Why is God allowing her to hang on when the person I knew disappeared years ago?"... He was still faithful, but the road was hard, the nights long, the loneliness intense, the future bleak.

Then my friend spent an evening with a man who told him, "You'll never know what you have meant to my son. He's been watching you take care of your wife all these years.... he's been talking about you to everyone he meets. He tells them that anyone else would have left her by now and started a new life. But you didn't do that. You stayed with her. And that has made a profound impression on my son."

—Ray Pritchard
The Road Best Traveled

I pray for a swift healing of your body and a rejuvenation of your spirit. I know how difficult this injury has been for you.

Even when the skies are grey, the sun continues to shine. Focus on the sun and not the clouds, for brighter days are coming. Get well soon.

May your path be made smooth and your spirit be lightened by the loving grace of a God who walks beside you.

In the midst of our suffering, we forget that we once felt whole and healthy and that we will be again. I pray you are on the swift road to recovery.

In the night sky, there is a star with light brighter than anything of this earth. It shines with his glorious light, beckoning you to join him in life's dance.

Because it is slow, healing is often not recognized. I remember when my husband was dying I kept a journal of my feelings on a tape recorder.... I carefully listened to the words in the early part of the tape. The words were words of despair and loneliness. Later the words began to sound more hopeful as new things were happening in my life. This was certainly a good tool to let me know that I was getting better.

—HELEN FITZGERALD
THE MOURNING HANDBOOK

Healing can come from many directions and in many forms. Wishing you the healing that will bring you comfort and strength.

Believe in yourself and your strength to see this through. I know that I believe in you!

You've never been one to ask for help, but there are so many people who want to show you how much they care. What can we do?

Life. The people you love and who love you. Your health. The job you have, the skill you have to do it, even the strength to do it. Each and every one of those things is a gift. Understanding that it is a gift makes you treasure the gift all the more, enjoy it all the more, and live life not only with a greater sense of appreciation but of indebtedness.

—KEN GIRE
WINDOWS OF THE SOUL

It's time to rest, repose, renew, relax, recharge, regroup, and before you know it, you'll be recuperated!

Even though I walk through the valley of the shadow of death, I will fear no evil, for you are with me.

PSALM 23:4 NIV

Prayer can be a powerful healer. Place yourself in God's hands.

You may not be able to control all that happens to your body, but you still have the healthiest mind I know.

I've hope to live, and am prepared to die.

—WILLIAM SHAKESPEARE
MEASURE FOR MEASURE

Out of pain, certain special qualities are born. Understanding, perseverance, sensitivity are invisible—yet, like any hidden treasure, invaluable....very often, times of pain become times when we get in touch with our own soul, perhaps as never before.

—JANE GRAYSHON
IN TIMES OF PAIN

May your health improve with each passing day as you get stronger and stronger!

I want to be there for you, to be with you, and to be involved. Please let me help!

Sometimes the greatest gift you can give is to ask for help.

Your courage has been an inspiration. You made it this far—you can do anything!

We hope you can feel our love and our prayers, for you are wrapped in our thoughts every moment.

You are my inspiration...
for your never-ending smile,
for maintaining your compassionate nature,
for your courage in never giving up the battle,
and for your strength in greeting each new day.

I am praying for you so very hard every day.

Loss of a Friend

Blessed are those who mourn, for they will be comforted.

MATTHEW 5:4 NIV

May all your great memories come to overshadow the sadness of loss.

Grief is not something to be smothered, and memories should not be covered up. The goal is to remember special people in our lives with love, reflecting on happy memories and not being afraid to cry when we feel once more the pain of their absence.

—HEATHER LEHR WAGNER
DEALING WITH TERMINAL ILLNESS IN THE FAMILY

This world is not conclusion;
A species stands beyond,
Invisible, as music,
But positive, as sound.

—EMILY DICKINSON

The goodness of her soul is shining on you right now.

The road through grief is shorter when shared with others. You can count on me to share the journey.

I have always heard it observed that Music and Play, will fright Sorrow away.

—MIGUEL DE CERVANTES
DON QUIXOTE

Memories come in all sizes.
Cherish them all, store them safely,
and let them become part of you.

Your friend endured so much that
we can find comfort in knowing
her suffering has ended.

Grief melts away
Like snow in May,
As if there were no such cold thing.

—George Herbert
"The Flower"

There is sadness in loss but peace
in knowing that suffering has ended
for your dear pet friend.

My heart, my prayers, and my love
go out to you in this time of
mourning.

I wish for you a healing of
the heart and spirit that you may
one day see the joy a new life has
to offer.

But if the while I think on thee,
  dear friend,
All losses are restored and
  sorrows end.

—William Shakespeare
Sonnet 30

Losing a pet is like saying goodbye to a beloved family member. May you find comfort in remembering the powerful bond of love, loyalty, and companionship you shared.

Please don't be afraid to reach out to me for help. I know you are hurting. Let me help you get through the pain.

Grief is itself a medicine, and bestowed
To improve the fortitude that bears the load,
To teach the wanderer, as his woes increase,
The path of Wisdom, all whose paths are peace.

—WILLIAM COWPER
"CHARITY"

I know the parting is so difficult and sad. Yet how lucky you were to have known such a wonderful friendship! Remember, and in that remembering may you find healing.

A friend is like a treasure map that leads us to new adventures. Even though your friend is gone, the map remains imprinted upon your heart.

Losing your good friend is heartbreaking. But just remember all the love, laughter, and light the two of you shared. That will live on forever.

Even though we all must mourn our losses, grieving does have an end. It is a season, not a permanent lodging; you won't have to have your mail sent there. The loss may always be with you, but the pain eases.

—PATSY CLAIRMONT
MENDING YOUR HEART IN A BROKEN WORLD

A family pet lives on in our hearts, our spirits, and our memories. I am so sorry for the loss of your beloved companion and friend.

Though your heart is breaking, love lives on.
Though your spirit is aching, hope lives on.
With the love of friends, and with God, you will get through this.

Without the process of mourning there can be no recovery. Any surgical patient will attest to the fact that before he was healed and felt well he endured varying degrees of pain. No patient can avoid that process. No bereaved person who has endured the death of a special person can avoid the process either.

—HARRIET SARNOFF SCHIFF
LIVING THROUGH MOURNING

I know how much you will miss your friend. Let me help you get through this time of grief.

Those with whom we choose to walk through life bless us in many ways. Remember those blessings now and in the days to come.

The grieving process always alters the mourner. Grief inevitably leads to new strengths. When you allow yourself to experience fully the subtle gradations of its colors and textures, grief adds to your personal richness and depth.

—DONALD A. TUBESING
KICKING YOUR STRESS HABITS

Take comfort in knowing you did everything you could.

Losing a friend feels as though the pain will never end. But with time that pain will turn to a loving remembrance of the joy you shared together.

Your friend touched many hearts and will be missed terribly. Please accept my heartfelt sympathy for your loss.

Death takes away. That's all there is to it. But grief gives back. By experiencing it, we are not simply eroded by pain. Rather, we become larger human beings, more compassionate, more aware, more able to help others, more able to help ourselves.

—CANDY LIGHTNER AND NANCY HATHAWAY
GIVING SORROW WORDS

May God's love wrap around your grieving heart like a gentle and healing blanket.

Your sweet friend is gone. I am so very sorry for your loss. Let your heart remember the joy as you grieve, and you will find the smile in your tears.

Dear friends are such an amazing blessing…and so very hard to lose. May you take comfort in the joy you shared with your dear friend.

Always remember, for memories will lift your heart and warm your soul.

You've lost a very special friend. I'm hoping that the memories of all the wonderful times you shared together over the years will bring you comfort now and in the days to come.

Pets become our friends and members of the family. They snuggle up right beside our heart. So sorry to hear of your loss of this precious companion.

A Family Parting

Through the loss of your parent, you will learn that many people care for you and your family.

⌒

Losing a sibling makes everyone in a family a little closer. May your shared memories live and bring comfort.

⌒

Losing a grandparent is like losing a trusted ally—a partner who is blind to your flaws. Please allow me to help fill the void.

⌒

Mysteries surround us and force us to ask "Why?" Yet all we can do is move forward. You are not alone in your sorrow.

You are the legacy of your grandparents, and they must have held their heads high whenever they thought of you.

⌒

We have to choose what to do with our dead: To die when they die. To live crippled. Or to forge, out of pain and memory, new adaptations. Through mourning we acknowledge that pain, feel that pain, live past it. Through mourning we let the dead go and take them in. Through mourning we come to accept the difficult changes that loss must bring—and then we begin to come to the end of mourning.

—JUDITH VIORST
NECESSARY LOSSES

Family keeps us going, makes us laugh, and drives us crazy. May your family bring you comfort as you mourn this sad loss.

The love of a parent is a powerful force that lives on and will continue to guide you throughout life. May that thought bring you comfort.

It's tragedies like this that help us put things into perspective and appreciate our lives. I'm so sorry you must endure this.

Open your heart to the warmth of family and friends. Open your soul to the prayers of those who care. You are loved so very much.

She must have been a wonderful person, because I see her in you.

'Tis held that sorrow makes us wise.

—ALFRED LORD TENNYSON
"IN MEMORIAM"

Great artists live on in the beauty of their work. The beauty of your parents lives on in you.

Even after this final goodbye is spoken and the last tears are shed, your heart will always be close to the dear departed.

There is nothing more human than to cry if you have lost a loved one; nothing more natural than to feel disappointment if you have failed at some important task, and nothing more understandable than to feel angry if someone hurts you or uses you. The open expression of feelings... is not only natural and human, but is also tremendously important. Honest grieving and feeling, even though sometimes very painful, promotes eventual emotional healing.

—John Preston
You Can Beat Depression

When you consider all that your father has given you, you can see how much of him lives on in you— and how it shows in your beauty and goodness.

There are no words to convey just how much I grieve for your loss. My most heartfelt prayers are with you and your family.

May your heart one day find joy again. May your spirit one day find peace. I share in your grief.

———

I know how much this is hurting you, and I wish I could share your sadness. Instead, let me share my friendship.

———

Your parents lived life to the fullest and their passing is a reminder to do the same.

———

I offer you my deepest sympathy and my shoulder to cry on. Please call me if you need me.

———

Hold fast to each other and to God's unceasing love at this tragic time of loss.

Still, we cry, pine, remember, and move restlessly about in our search to recover someone we have lost and cannot find—much as children do. Like children, too, we then vent rage, anger, sadness, and despair until, finally, the intensity of all these emotions diminishes. The realization sinks in that reality will not change, and so we must change instead, reordering both our lives and our attachments. Child or adult, this is the journey of grief.

—Diane Cole
After Great Pain

———

Comfort comes in many forms— a happy time unexpectedly remembered, the hug of a dear friend, a child's smile, laughter from across the room. Be open to these special moments.

In love's loss we grieve, and somewhere deep within our pain We find a tiny seed of promise that our hearts will love again.

Losing someone you love is the greatest loss a heart can endure. You have my sympathy, my prayers, and my offer of comfort should you need me in any way.

I loved Susy, loved her dearly; but I did not know how deeply, before....Hour by hour my sense of the calamity that has over-taken us closes down heavier & heavier upon me....But though my heart *break* I will still say she was fortunate; & I would not call her back if I could.

—MARK TWAIN
THE LOVE LETTERS OF MARK TWAIN

May God dry your tears with the soothing touch of his love and heal your grief with his gentle presence.

Allow the rainbow of memories to bring a touch of light to your sorrow.

No words I can say will lessen the grief you must be feeling. Just know that I care and that I am only a phone call away.

God is with you in your sorrow as he was with you in your joy. May your faith bring you comfort.

Life can go from joy to despair in a moment's notice. But know that it can also go from despair to joy in time. My prayers are with you now.

I brushed the tears off my cheeks. Peace, like the warm afternoon sun, bathed my soul. Somehow I knew…heaven will be one place where parents don't cry.

—LILLIAN SPARKS
PARENTS CRY TOO

Lives of great men all remind us
We can make our lives sublime,
And, departing, leave behind us
Footprints on the sands of time;

Footprints, that perhaps another,
Sailing o'er life's solemn main
A forlorn and shipwrecked brother,
Seeing, shall take heart again.

Let us, then, be up and doing,
With a heart for any fate;
Still achieving, still pursuing,
Learn to labor and to wait.

—HENRY WADSWORTH LONGFELLOW
"A PSALM OF LIFE"

To lose someone you love is hard. May you find courage from loving memories, strength in the light of each new day, and comfort in the love and kindness of family and friends.

Let time be your companion, guiding you gently to that moment when grief turns to memory and sorrow becomes the fullness of appreciation for all that you shared.

A Family Parting 〜 67

Though we still miss them, we experience the pain of missing them differently. It is no longer simply a bitterness at deprivation. It becomes a unique pain in separation that we can more easily carry. Yes, we have lost their physical presence. But not all is lost. They have already begun to occupy a different place in our lives. The richness of lasting love consoles us. We miss them even as we cherish their legacies, enjoy the fruition of their lives, and live in gratitude for all they have given and continue to give.

—THOMAS ATTIG
THE HEART OF GRIEF

Don't count the hours you missed. Hold tight to the precious ones you shared.

Feel the strength in this day and the promise of a time when the sorrow will fade and you will smile once again.

Losing family is so hard—even if the loss was expected. God be with you.

It's easy to get angry at life for taking from us those we love. But try to let memories remind you of the blessings God provided by giving you such an amazing relative.

Your beloved child left you far too early, but your child gave you a lifetime's worth of joy.

There is no sad time in life that doesn't contain at least a hint of hope. It doesn't appear immediately when you're mourning a great loss, but if you look for it, it's there.

—Delilah
Love Someone Today

Our parents are only ours for a short time, and they are eventually called home to God.

While I can't tell you when you will recover from grief, I can assure you that people *do* recover. And while some sadness will always be there, the tears and grief will become more manageable as you integrate them into your life and live with them. I do know that the intense pain of early grief goes away after a while, leaving an ache that will also subside. I know countless people who have had to endure shocking, devastating losses and yet have gone on to live happy and productive lives.

—Helen Fitzgerald
The Mourning Handbook

Remember that where there is now grief, there once was love and laughter that will continue to live on in your heart.

A Spouse's Departure

Wherever your loved one may be: the greater the love, the shorter the distance.

Laughter *will* come again, and it's important that you embrace it. Don't feel guilty the first time you laugh again—even if it is during this time of deep sorrow and grief. Laughing, like tears, can be an emotional release, and your loved one would be pleased to know you are adjusting to life.

—FAYE LANDRUM
THE FINAL MILE

Please don't let your loss give way to loneliness. I'm here for you whenever you need to talk.

One promises to love "until death do us part" without realizing that we love long after that.

We will take a moment to think of you and your loved one each and every day.

In time, yesterday's sorrow turns to peace.

Your wife would insist that you think happy thoughts. May they come easily.

Your husband fought for life with courage and grace. May we live on with the same qualities.

May tomorrow be filled with only your happiest memories.

After so many years, you have a wealth of memories to embrace and again feel his presence.

To weep is to make less the depth of grief.

—WILLIAM SHAKESPEARE
THE THIRD PART OF HENRY VI

Losing a spouse feels like losing half of your heart and soul. I am here, friend, if you need me. Let me help you get through this.

I wish I could say just the right words to take away your suffering, but instead I'll just say that I care for you and that I'm here for you.

Reaching the avenue of acceptance is a road fraught with twisting and turning bypaths. It is not easy. You may place a smile on your face but your heart will still hurt because your special person is gone. Ultimately you will reach some inner peace, but that is not how it begins: it begins with the attempts.

—HARRIET SARNOFF SCHIFF
LIVING THROUGH MOURNING

You have lost the one who meant the most to you, but love never dies. It is simply transformed into something far grander than we can imagine.

The love you shared has not ended but transformed into a heartful of treasured memories. Let those memories comfort you now in this time of suffering.

It is unrealistic to expect any grief to be an orderly process.... expect setbacks. The ebb and flow of emotions lends itself to discovery of unresolved pockets of grief. You may uncover a gaping hole just when you think the wound is almost healed.

Don't allow yourself to become discouraged when this happens. Call a trusted friend and discuss what you are experiencing, even if you think the person is tired of hearing you talk about your grief. Talking about your pain is an effective method of healing.

—DAVID COX & CANDY ARRINGTON
AFTERSHOCK

I cannot share your loss, but I can share your pain. Let me be of help in any way I can.

Let love clasp Grief lest both be drown'd.

—ALFRED LORD TENNYSON
"IN MEMORIAM"

I pray that the light of God's love leads you out of the darkness and back into the joy of life again.

All of us who experience the suffering of loss undergo great changes. We are healed in different ways by these changes, and we eventually reconstruct our lives. Resolving sorrow means being able to express it and putting it into a place inside us, weaving it in our lives as a thread in a complex and rich tapestry.

—MARGUERITE BOUVARD,
WITH EVELYN GLADU
THE PATH THROUGH GRIEF

To love means there is sorrow at the loss of love. With sorrow there grows the healing warmth of memories. In memories may you find great comfort.

Nothing will be the same. It's true, but you *will* find a way through this, and there *will* be laughter in your world once again.

If the pain gets to be too much to bear, know that I will be there to help you get through it in any way I can.

Losing a loving companion is more than the heart can bear alone. Please don't hesitate to come to me for support should you need someone to lean on.

A Spouse's Departure ━

There is no greater loss than that of a beloved partner in life. When you're ready to reach out, know that I'll be ready to help you heal.

In your grief, remember that you are deeply cared for by God, family, and friends.

Though your heart is breaking, know that God's love can bring you happiness in time. I pray for you daily.

Always remember that your love will never die. It is a part of you— now and always.

To have known a love like yours is one of the greatest blessings the Lord can bestow.

My heart goes out to you in this time of mourning. My loving prayers surround you in this time of grief.

Whether you choose to visit the cemetery, write in a journal, or make a contribution to a worthy cause in your loved one's name, it is essential to find a way to acknowledge the loss you have suffered and the love you have experienced. It is comforting to know that the feelings of loss will fade. The feelings of love will not.

—CANDY LIGHTNER AND NANCY HATHAWAY
GIVING SORROW WORDS

May you find healing and comfort in the warmth of loving memories.

A life has ended, but the loving memory of that precious life will remain forever in our hearts and minds.

We send our sympathies to you and your family during this time of mourning. Your loss is felt in our hearts, and we pray that you will find comfort.

I know you must feel so alone. But you are never alone. I am here for you, and so is the one who loves you most of all—God.

What can I say? I just want you to know that I am holding you close in thought and prayer, hoping with all my heart that you know that you are not alone.

There is never enough time to love. We just have to savor the memories of the time we were given. Thinking of you with all my heart.

Take time to recall and rejoice in the progress you've made since that moment when someone you loved died. Call back the memories of the good times and the great times. And if there were trying, soul-wrenching and horrifying times, perhaps as you witnessed your loved one slowly, even painfully move to the final transition to death, put these experiences in among the many displaying in your own kaleidoscope of life.

—EVA SHAW
WHAT TO DO WHEN A LOVED ONE DIES

Many lives were touched by the love you shared, and all of us are holding you in our thoughts, wishing there was something we could do to help.

In all human sorrows nothing gives comfort but love and faith.

—LEO TOLSTOY
ANNA KARENINA

God gave you such an amazing gift in the love that you shared. Hold onto that love, and hold onto the Lord, for in these you will find comfort and peace.

Even though prayer cannot erase the tragedy of your loss, may it help ease your heartache and hasten the time when tears come less often. I am praying for you.

May God give you the strength and courage you will need, and may the love of those surrounding you help provide comfort and rest.

The family you created together is a living legacy to the love you have shared. May you find comfort and joy in your children at this very difficult time.

Let the grief wash over you like a cleansing rain as you slowly take steps toward a new life—rich in beautiful, loving memories.

Partners in life … partners for always. The love and delight you two shared will forever be a part of you.

Sorrow will lead you through this time. Allow it its due that you may emerge from the sadness to a place of comfort and acceptance.

Losing your partner is extremely difficult. There's nothing that could ever prepare you. What can you do? Be patient, for time will lift the weight of loss. Truly, it will.

Let the tears and sadness take you through your grief to ease the heartache as you slowly see the dawn of a new day.

A Spouse's Departure — 77